THE TOP-NOTCH NANNIES' GUIDE

JEAN AND JASMINE BIRTLES

CARTOONS BY NOEL KELLY

SUMMERSDALE

Copyright © Jean and Jasmine Birtles 1996

All rights reserved.

No part of this book may be reproduced by any means, nor transmitted, nor translated into a machine language, without the written permission of the publisher.

Summersdale Publishers
46 West Street
Chichester
West Sussex
PO19 1RP

A CIP catalogue record for this book is available from the British Library.

Printed in Great Britain.

ISBN 1 873475 85 3

BIG THANKS TO.....Top Notch Nanny Melanie Nesbitt and her charge Charlie for being our supermodels on the front cover, Elaine Mercer for her quiet brilliance, CACHE, NAMCW, Chiltern College, Norland College, The Isle College and all the other course-providers for helping us with information, Steve Woods for his photography and Della Drees at '3's Company' for making the book cover so attractive.

CONTENTS

1. INTRODUCTION..5
2. NANNY, NURSIE, AU-PAIR, MUM - WHAT ARE THEY?..........................10
3. INTERVIEWING NANNIES..........................15
4. DAY TO DAY LIFE WITH A NANNY..........34
5. THE CONTRACT..44
6. MALE NANNIES..49
7. AU-PAIRS...51
8. MATERNITY NURSES..61
9. WHY USE AN AGENCY?.......................................67
10. DON'T!...74
11. NANNY TAX AND NATIONAL INSURANCE..........................76
12. GET CAMPAIGNING...83
13. ABOUT TOP-NOTCH NANNIES.....................86

USEFUL NAMES AND ADDRESSES......................88

RECOMMENDED READING..91

CHAPTER 1

INTRODUCTION

*"People who say they sleep like babies
usually don't have one."*
Moyra Bremner.

When we think of nannies we usually think of someone cosy and motherly - even grandmotherly: someone like Mary Poppins, Madam Doubtfire or the nannies who were loved by people like Joyce Grenfell and Christopher Robin Milne.

But nannies have changed a lot in the last twenty years. Now, they are usually young, anything from 18 to early 30's, and they generally enjoy life, have boyfriends, go out and socialise and expect to get married and have their own children some time. There are also now a few male nannies and quite a number of nannies from overseas.

The profession has also become more businesslike. Nannying is taught in colleges all over the country and many employers feel that experience on its own is just not enough. Many even want someone who qualified at a specific college.

Hiring nannies has changed a great deal too. In the era of Upstairs Downstairs hiring a nanny was comparatively simple. Many were handed down through generations. Some members of the royal family still continue that practice. Prince Charles's nanny, Helen Lightbody, had previously cared for the Duke and Duchess of Gloucester's two sons. The Queen's nannies 'Bobo' Macdonald and her sister Ruby, became part of the family, attending Prince Charles's christening.

Nowadays, with nannies coming in all shapes and sizes, the whole area is something of a minefield. The hand that rocks the cradle can rock the whole house so you should approach the whole business as exactly that - a piece of business and a very important one too.

As we all know, children are like sponges and will absorb the thoughts and behaviour of those who are around them. If we want our children to be healthy, happy and normal we need to make sure that they are surrounded by people who can help them become that way. In this book we hope to give you all the information you need to find just the right nanny or other carer for the most important little people in your life.

CAN I AFFORD A NANNY?

Before you start looking for a nanny you need to do your sums. Nannies are expensive whichever way you look at it. The demand for good nannies and other child-carers far outstrips the supply so if you want a really good, experienced and qualified nanny you are going to have to be prepared to pay for one. In London nannies know that they could earn £80 a day gross if they worked in a nursery which gives you an idea of what you are competing with! However, in childcare, just as in many other professions, if you pay peanuts you get monkeys - and who wants a monkey to potty-train their baby? We can't stress enough the importance of going for the best nanny or childminder you can afford.

You will have to pay the nanny out of your *net* pay and there is no tax relief for privately-arranged childcare yet (see page 83 for details of tax relief pressure groups). The chart below gives you a rough idea of how much your nanny will cost you in total.

Nanny net weekly pay	Your gross weekly cost	Gross cost per annum
£100	£120	£ 6,300
£150	£206	£10,700
£200	£297	£15,400
£250	£382	£19,900

This may look expensive, but if you are working and you want your child to be cared for by someone who has experience and has trained for it for over a year a nanny is the only possible option. This is one area of life in which you should not try to save pennies. (For a fuller explanation of exactly how much a nanny will cost you, you could contact Nannytax - their phone number is at the end of the book).

Childminders are certainly cheaper than nannies but you have to take the child to the minder and pick him or her up every day and your child will often be looked after with the childminder's own. This could be fun or it could mean that your child is ignored at times in favour of her own. Many parents also worry about the calibre of childminders as they are usually completely untrained and are not always checked thoroughly enough.

And then there are nurseries. Again, it depends on your lifestyle and the type of child you have whether you would prefer to send your child to a nursery rather than having him or her cared for at home. Nurseries vary in price depending on where they are and what facilities they have but, as with nannies, it is important to check them out very carefully and speak to other parents who send their children there before leaving yours in their hands. We are not dealing with nurseries in this book but *The Good Nursery Guide (Vermillion)* is a useful book to read if you are considering that option.

Of course there are other options but they should only be considered if your child is old enough, if they fit in with your lifestyle and you don't necessarily want your child to be cared for at home. For example, an au pair will only cost you about £45 a week (cash) and does not need to pay tax or National Insurance. But you must remember that au pairs are young, inexperienced, untrained and have, at best, just a working knowledge of English. Also they are not supposed to work for any more than 25 hours a week and should not be allowed sole charge of a child under two and a half. If you have a baby or a toddler you should never allow an au pair to look after it on her own.

If, having done your sums, you feel you can't afford the type of paid childcare that you feel would be best for your little one, then arrange with your partner for one of you to stay home or for you both to work part-time. For your peace of mind and the health and safety of your child it is not worth going for someone sub-standard to look after your baby. Better to stay at home than worry in the office. We have all heard too many horror stories of children, and sometimes parents, being abused by cheap 'minders' who were hired without care to take any aspect of the business lightly. Finding the best childcare for your family is a very serious business and there is no room to cut corners.

CHAPTER 2

NANNY, NURSIE, AU PAIR, MUM - WHAT ARE THEY?

*"Before I had kids I went home after work to rest.
Now I go to work to rest."*
Simon Ruddell.

If you are new to the world of nannies and other child-carers you may be wondering what all the terms mean. What is the difference between a nanny and a maternity nurse? What is a mother's help? What does an au pair do?

Basically it is down to qualifications, experience, levels of responsibility and hours of work that each job requires. Briefly, here are some definitions to help you decide what sort of help you need with your children.

A NANNY

A nanny is aged from 18 years upwards and is usually female although there are a few male nannies around now (See page 49). Nannies can be qualified, having done a two year college course and gained an N.N.E.B., N.A.N.C.W., BTEC, NVQ or similar certificates or they can can be a former Mother's Help with several years' experience but no formal qualifications.

A nanny's prime, and sometimes only, duty is to look after the children and their belongings. This usually includes washing, ironing and cooking for them (and for them *only*) as well as cleaning their nurseries and/or bedrooms, not forgetting her own. She will not do general household duties other than those to do with the children. If the nanny lives in she will have her own bedroom and often a private bathroom. Some nannies have their own self-contained apartments and many are given a car or the use of the family's car.

A nanny's wage depends on qualifications, experience, age and whether she lives in or out. In London and the

Home Counties nannies generally earn a *net* weekly salary of between £120-£250 or more (you pay her tax and national insurance contributions on top of that). In the rest of the country they are a bit cheaper. Nannies who live in are paid less than those living out but that's because they get a room and full board. Some employers offer travelling expenses for daily nannies (that's nannies who live out).

A nanny should not work for more than ten hours a day although she can be expected to baby-sit two evenings a week. She should have a minimum of one and a half days off per week which would include one full day completely free. Most nannies expect at least two full days off per week.

You could have a 'nanny share' where you share a nanny with another family and meet the costs together. Under the 1989 Children Act nannies must be registered by the local authority if they look after children from more than two families in the same place at the same time. However, most nanny shares involve just two families, often where one family has the nanny to live in and therefore pays her less than the other one.

A MOTHER'S HELP

A mother's help is usually 16-years-old or more. She has no formal training but may have had experience of this work before and/or comes from a large family and is used to helping in the home. She might have done a childcare course at school which involved helping out at local playschools and some practical experience with small babies.

A mother's help will assist the mother or father in caring for the children. If she's experienced and confident enough she can take sole charge of the children at times. Unlike nannies, mother's helps will do some light housework (dusting, vacuuming etc.).

A mother's help earns a *net* weekly salary of between £110-£200 a week depending on her experience and whether the position is live in or out. Some employers also offer travelling expenses if the position is live-out. If living-in the mother's help would expect her own room and to live as one of the family where possible.

A mother's help should not work for more than ten hours a day. The working week should include at least one and a half days off including one full day free and at least three evenings off. Bank holidays should be given or days off in lieu and holidays are negotiable although, as with nannies, two to four weeks a year is the norm.

AU PAIRS

Many people get confused between nannies and au pairs but there is a world of difference between them.

Unlike nannies, au pairs have no formal training in caring for children and most have little experience of it. Au pairs are foreign (see page 52 for the list of nationalities who are allowed to be au pairs) and their main reason for being in this country is to learn the language and enjoy some of the British culture.

Au pairs are not nanny substitutes. They are unqualified, often inexperienced, girls or boys of between 18-27 years of age. Home Office rules state that au pairs can only work 25 hours a week with a couple of evenings a week for babysitting and all their weekends free. They are only supposed to do *light* housework and should not have sole charge of the children. Au pairs are certainly cheap but in the field of childcare you get what you pay for!

MATERNITY NURSES

Most maternity nurses are interested in babies only and will expect to work for you for just a couple of months after you have given birth. They are generally highly-trained and have a particular love for, and understanding of babies and for this you pay between £250-500 a week (another reason why she will probably only work for you for a short time!). Maternity nurses are particularly useful if you have had a difficult birth. They are also helpful if you have had your first child as they can teach you a great deal about caring for babies in a short time.

One very important thing you need to know about maternity nurses is that they are all booked up all the time. Booking a maternity nurse is like putting your son down for Eton. You practically have to get hold of one the day after the child's conceived to be sure of employing her!

CHAPTER 3

INTERVIEWING NANNIES

"Nannying is a profession just like medicine or the law, although if you have several children to care for it's more like being an air traffic controller."
Jasmine Birtles

If you have contacted a nanny through an agency much of the work will have been done for you. The agency will have collated her CV, references, certificates and other details and *should* have checked at least two of her references by phone or letter. We always check at least two references, and often three, by phone because occasionally girls will make some up and might even ask friends to pretend to be a former employer. However, you can often spot the deception by careful questioning over the phone.

Whether or not you have contacted the nanny through an agency, though, you should check her references yourself. You can find out a lot about the character of a girl by asking a former employer what she was really like.

You may even find that although the girl suited the other employer, what she says about her shows you that she would not suit you.

At the moment there is no national register of nannies, although a register has been started by some agencies who belong to FRES. If you would like details contact them on the number given on page 88. Otherwise, unless they have been convicted of a major crime, it is almost impossible to find out anything about someone by doing a police check on them. So the only way you can be sure of a new nanny is by thoroughly checking all her references and trusting your gut feeling when you interview her.

THE INTERVIEW

This is your big chance to avoid possible misery later on so don't allow fear, shyness or lack of time stop you from getting an accurate picture of each applicant. If necessary write down a list of questions you think are important before you meet her. If you are not sure what questions are relevant here is a list to give you an idea:

1. Ask her about her last job: how long was she there and why did she leave?

2. Ask to see references and make sure they have phone numbers and addresses so that you can check them.

3. Ask her about her training: what subjects did she cover and how long did she study? Make sure she has her original certificates, not photocopies.

4. To what level did she study? Advanced, Ordinary, Foundation?

5. Has she worked with children of the same age as yours before?

6. Can she prepare simple, healthy food for the children and herself?

7. Does she have lots of ideas for entertaining your children?

8. Does she have any first aid training? If not, would she be prepared to attend an evening training session if you could find one?

9. Does she smoke?

10. Does she have any special dietary needs?

11. If you have pets does she get on with them? Is she allergic to them?

12. Is she musical? Can she sing, play the guitar or piano? Would she be happy to sing with the children, teach them songs, teach them to play a little?

13. Does she swim? Would she be prepared to take your children swimming each week?

14. How does she think children should be disciplined?

15. Does she drive? If so does she have a car or would she expect one to be provided?

16. If you ever considered a nanny share would she be happy to look after someone else's child for a few days a week?

17. Is she happy to help with household chores?

18. If she is a live-out nanny, how far away does she live and how long did it take her to get to you? If she came by tube or train, is there an alternative bus route if there is a strike?

19. Does she have any dependants?

20. Does she have a boyfriend or fiancé? How will he fit into her life in your home? Does he live nearby?

21. Is she alert to possible dangers in the home? Describe a few hypothetical emergency situations to her and ask how she would deal with them.

22. How much babysitting is she willing to do? (If she is living in, two nights' babysitting is usually considered part of the job.) If she is living out, will she be available for babysitting, and what hourly rate can you agree on together?

23. Would she be happy to come back for a second interview when you have seen all the applicants?

24. Will she come on holiday with you if you want her to?

Of course, job interviews are two-way streets. The nanny will be assessing you and your children and home as much as you are assessing her. If she is professional and sensible she will probably have a number of questions for you. She may ask questions like these:

1. Why did your last nanny leave? How long was she with you?

2. What are the hours I will have to work?

3. What happens in the case of illness? Do you offer sick pay?

4. Will you be paying my tax and national insurance?

5. Will I have sole charge of the children?

6. Will I be expected to do any cleaning, ironing or other housework?

7. Will you want me to babysit?

8. If I am living in, will I be able to invite friends and boyfriends round?

9. If I am living out, will you pay my travel expenses?

Before the interview, you may find it useful to write down a list of points about the job that the nanny should know so that she can see if the job is right for her. For example, if you have specific foods or drinks that you will not allow in the house she ought to know; similarly if you want someone who could work two Sunday's a month (with time off during the week) she should also know that at the interview.

It's important that the applicant meets your children too. You can tell very quickly how she feels about them from the way she behaves towards them at the first meeting. If she is genuinely a child-lover she will immediately try to make friends, or at least show some interest in them. The children, too, will be able to tell you what they think of the applicant if they are toddlers or older.

Remember: BE HONEST! There is no point pretending that the job is easy and that she'll get lots of time off and regular bonuses if this is not going to happen. Once she realises what the job is really like she will be off faster than you can say 'Top-Notch Nanny' and you will have to go through the whole rigmarole again. If you *are* honest and no one takes the job you may have to reassess the salary you are offering. It is likely that for the duties and hours you are demanding, the pay is just not enough. Sorry, but it is a nanny's market at the moment and they can afford to pick and choose, so if you are expecting her to care for the twins from 7 till 7, babysit four times a week and only take one day off at the weekend all for just £100 a week you will have big problems finding the right help!

QUALIFICATIONS: WHAT THEY MEAN

There are so many childcare qualifications around now that it can be very confusing to see a girl's certificates and try to work out what they mean. It is important to have some idea, though, because some courses last three years and involve a great deal of practical work and others can be just six weeks or a short course of evening classes. If you are not sure what some qualifications mean ask the girl to explain what she did on the course, how long it took, how much practical experience it included and if it counts as an NVQ (National Vocational Qualification).

Courses are changing all the time as nannying becomes more and more professional. However, as a rough guide here is a brief description of some of the main nanny and childcare qualifications your applicant may have:

B/TEC

The Business and Technical Council qualification is the highest any nanny can achieve although it is not as well-known in the private sector as the NNEB qualifications. It is taken by the more academic 16-year-olds and is seen as being equal to two 'A'levels. It covers all the same ground that the NNEB does but to a more academic level.

BTEC offers courses in Caring Services (Nursery Nursing) at two levels: *First* and *National*. The *First* courses in Caring provide students with a foundation for a range of careers including Nursery Nursing. If a student takes five modules she qualifies for a Certificate. If they take eight they qualify for a Diploma. Compulsory subjects for all students are Behavioural and Community Studies, Common Skills Assignments, and Data Collection and Interpretation. Optional subjects that students can choose from are Biology, Caring Skills, First Aid, Health Education, Human Development and Investigative Assignments. Those taking the Diploma have to do at least 150-180 hours of work experience placements.

The *National* Certificate and Diploma in Caring Services (Nursery Nursing) provide students with the skills, knowledge and understanding to enable immediate and effective employment as a nursery nurse. The Certificate comprises a minimum of ten units and the Diploma a minimum of 16 units. Each qualification is based around seven core subjects: Child Care - Care of the Sick Child; Child Care - Practice and Services; Common Skills A (Year 1); Common Skills B (Year 2); Community Assignment; Data Investigation; Human Growth and Development; Learning Activities A.

The optional subjects from which students may choose are: Core Science; Data Interpretation; Early Childhood Education; First Aid and Safety; Health Education; Home Environment Studies; Learning Activities B; Legal Aspects of Nursery Nursing; Psychological Aspects of Child Development; Sociological Aspects of Child Development; Special Needs. The National Courses teach students to an NVQ Level 3.

In both the First and National Courses, a large percentage of time is spent in work experience placements.

N.N.E.B.

In 1994 the National Nursery Examination Board (NNEB) merged with the Council for Early Years Awards (CEYA) and became CACHE (The Council for Awards in Children's Care and Education). CACHE offers a range of qualifications in childcare including the NNEB (now called the Diploma in Nursery Nursing) and National Vocational Qualifications (NVQs).

As the NNEB qualification is so widely known and respected, CACHE are happy to continue referring to the new diploma as the NNEB, although that is not strictly its proper name. The Diploma in Nursery Nursing (NNEB) gives would-be child carers a thorough grounding in most aspects of childcare from 0-8 years. The course takes two years and includes six terms of work in which students cover 20 modules, each of which is assessed by an assignment or a test. Students can be awarded 'distinctions' in various modules so you can find out if an applicant was a star pupil by counting these up. On some courses it is also possible to be assessed for an NVQ in Child Care and Education at Level 2 or 3.

Forty per cent of the course is practical work, including placements in nurseries or in private homes. Applicants also learn how to plan activities to entertain children, how to help them develop and how to care for their physical needs including hygiene, first aid and safety. Other parts of the course include Emotional and Social Development, Language Development, Food and Nutrition, Work with Babies of 0 - 1 years old, Child Protection, Good Practice of a Nursery Nurse, Helping Children with Special Needs, Working with Parents, and the Social and Legal Framework for Children and Families.

CACHE also offers the Certificate in Child Care and Education (CCE) which consists of 14 modules, 12 core plus two options, and takes one year to complete. The two main areas covered by the course are Knowledge and Understanding, and Practical Skills and Competency. The 12 core modules are Equality of Opportunity, The Care and Education Environment, Child Safety, Physical Care of the Developing Child, Provision of Food and Drinks,

Childhood Illness, Working with Young Children, Play and the Young Child, Emotional and Social Development, Parents and Carers, Managing Children's Behaviour, and Early Years Services. Students who take the CCE may be able to be assessed for NVQ Level 2.

For those looking for professional development CACHE offers an Advanced Diploma in Child Care and Education (ADCE). If you meet an applicant who has this qualification you should consider her very seriously. Only students who already have an NNEB or equivalent, or an NVQ Level 3 may study for this diploma. It takes a year to complete and involves six modules - one of which is a dissertation. Among the module choices are Language and Literacy, Disability/Special Needs, Children and Families Under Stress, Management of Early Years Provision and Child Protection.

There have been many changes in the NNEB course and awards over the years so if you want to check a qualification ring CACHE on the number given on page 88 under Useful Names and Addresses.

Candidates can take the Diploma in Nursery Nusing (NNEB) course at local authority colleges or sixth form colleges, but those with money (or who win a scholarship) can take it at one of the few residential colleges. In addition to following the Diploma in Nursery Nursing (NNEB) course, each private college adds its own slant on the training of nannies and you will find that graduates of a particular college will have similar approaches to the job. The four main residential colleges are Norland, Chiltern, Princess Christian and Montessori.

NORLAND

The Norland College in Berkshire is the most famous of the four. Graduates of the college have a distinctive uniform of brown and beige and many parents like to have a Norland nanny (often in her uniform) for snob value. However, the college's teaching standards are generally considered to be excellent, anyway.

The college has its own nursery with three classes, three day-care units and a children's hotel which local children attend and in which the students receive some of their practical experience. It also offers a 24-hour service for parents who would like to leave their child there for short periods thus giving the students even more experience.

As well as covering all the subjects required for the Diploma in Nursery Nursing (NNEB) offered by CACHE, all students spend three months in a hospital working in the paediatric, maternity or special care baby units.

A unique aspect of the Norland attitude to nannying is that once a student has passed all the relevant exams she is only described as a 'Probationer'. The college's in-house agency will place her with an approved family, day nursery or nursery school on this basis and not until she has completed twelve months of satisfactory work can she receive the Norland diploma and badge. After that she is considered a fully-fledged nanny, able to command a full salary.

CHILTERN

Chiltern College is also in Berkshire and also has an on-site nursery which caters for children from the age of six weeks. It has a Nursery School and a Primary School for 5 to 11 year-olds and runs some children's activity clubs during the holidays. After school care and a Holiday Club are also provided. All the students take part in the nursery and the school which give them excellent practical experience. They also gain valuable experience through placements in local families with a new baby, special needs placements and positions in local schools.

The college has admitted a few men in recent years and has seen them successfully employed after graduating and hopes to expand this area of training in the future. It has also welcomed several foreign students, most recently a number of girls from Eastern Europe who have been sponsored by Government-run charities.

Chiltern nannies have their own uniform in smart navy and royal blue with black lace-up moccasins. This gives them a traditional nanny image.

Employers of Chiltern nannies find that their broadly based training equips them well for the pressurised life of a nanny and that they are generally down-to-earth and highly competant workers.

PRINCESS CHRISTIAN

This residential college is in Manchester and, again, incorporates a day nursery and nursery school, including baby units, which are used by local parents and where the students gain valuable practical experience. Graduates of the college are issued with a Testimonial Book which has blank pages so that future employer's references can be kept in one place. The college keeps in touch with its graduates and awards a badge to nannies who have completed five years of nannying.

Employers generally find that Princess Christian nannies are practical with a friendly but efficient manner.

MONTESSORI

Montessori-trained nannies are unique in that they study not only for the NNEB qualification but also the Montessori Childcare and Teaching Diploma. The Montessori method is based on the concept of teaching as 'directing' children's own ability to find things out for themselves at their own pace.

The London Montessori Centre has an on-site nursery and it also has a Student Nanny Certificate which involves a student living with a family who pay her £70 a week to work for them 42 hours a week and she works at the Centre three mornings a week. This lasts for a year, after which she may do the NNEB course.

SCOTVEC

In Scotland the SCOTVEC National Certificate courses are similar to the English Diploma in Nursery Nursing (NNEB). Like the CACHE awards they consist of a combination of theoretical and practical work. The programme of SCOTVEC modules leads to a national certificate as well as a higher national certificate.

NVQs/SVQs in Child Care and Education at Levels 2 and 3 are recent additions to the range of qualifications would-be nannies can receive. At Level 2 the units covered are: Work with Babies; Work in Support of Others; Work in Pre-school Groups and Work in Community-run Pre-school Groups. Level 3 covers: Group Care and Education; Family Day Care; Pre-school Provision; Family Support and Special Needs.

THE ISLE COLLEGE

This college in Cambridgeshire offers a few courses for would-be nannies. They offer the B/TEC Childhood Studies Nursery Nursing Diploma which takes two years full-time and includes all the aspects of the course described above. The B/TEC Certificate takes one year to complete (see above for more details).

They also offer their own College Certificate plus NAMCW Stage 3 which takes one year to complete and also includes study for the St Johns Public First Aid Certificate, the Royal Institute of Public Health and Hygiene Primary Certificate in Food Hygiene, English Speaking Board Spoken English Certificate for Nursery Nurses and Word Power - Stages 1-3 as appropriate. This course gives students the knowledge and understanding necessary to undertake a Level Two NVQ in Childcare and Education. This course is especially designed for students who would like to work in private households.

Both courses include a lot of practical experience including at least one placement in a private home.

LUCY CLAYTON

The Lucy Clayton College in London has just introduced a one-year Certificate in Child Care and Education. There are 12 core modules that are compulsory and one extra Option Module. The compulsory subjects are: Equality of Opportunity; The Care and Education Environment; Child Safety; Physical Care of the Developing Child; Provision of Food and Drinks; Childhood Illness; Working with Young Children; Play and the Young Child; Emotional and Social Development; Parents and Carers; Managing Children's Behaviour; Early Years Services. Optional subjects are Caring for babies 6 weeks to 1 year or Feeding babies 6 weeks to 1 year. The course also includes a fully certificated St John's First Aid course.

Lucy Clayton also offer a twelve week nannying course which gives students a basic knowledge of childcare, and Babysitting and Childminding courses which last one week. Someone with this training will make a tip-top babysitter but is certainly not a nanny!

CITY AND GUILDS

City and Guilds do various certificates which can form a good basis for nannying or caring for the elderly or infirm. A suitable qualification for Childcare is the City and Guilds Childcare and Education NVQ (3034). This generally takes two years and is almost all based on job experience rather than classroom learning. Useful modules for this NVQ include:

- special needs
- work with babies
- family support

For further details on City and Guilds' range of courses for the care sector you can contact the number on page 88 under Useful Names and Addresses.

NAMCW

The NAMCW offer two programmes of study for would-be nannies: the NAMCW Advanced Certificate in Child Care and Education and NAMCW Diploma in Nursery Nursing. Both programmes have been completely re-written and updated in 1996. The Advanced Certificate is a one year course comprised of 17 modules including Welfare of Young Children, Co-operating With Other Carers, Special Needs and Developing a Stimulating, Child-centred Environment. The course now covers the knowledge requirements for the NVQ Standards at Level Two. The Diploma is a two year course comprising 12 units including The Sick Child, Learning Activities, First Aid, Health and Safety Education and Child Care Practice and Services. It now covers the knowledge requirements for the NVQ Standards at Level Three. Both programmes include 2 days per week spent on practical experience in the work place. Candidates will have practical, assessed experience of children aged 0-2 years, 2-4 years and 4-8 years including children with special needs. The NAMCW programmes can be seen as an alternative developed specifically to support candidates wishing to progress to assessment of NVQ.

PCSC

The Preliminary Certificate in Social Care is a type of foundation course for 16-19 year-olds who want to work in some form of residential care. It is a full-time, two-year course and includes teaching on how to work with children and other types of care. An applicant who just has this qualification and very little experience should only be considered as a mother's help.

WHAT TO LOOK FOR IN A NANNY

....very much depends on what you like.

Nannies come in all shapes and sizes and, being human, they have varying characters. What you *won't* find unless you are very lucky (or unlucky depending upon your point of view) is the traditional 'old dear' who lives only for the children, has a strict routine and whose idea of a good evening's entertainment is listening to the Archer's with a cup of cocoa, while darning the children's clothes.

Modern nannies tend to see the job as a short-term career. Many give it up if they get married or have children. Very few expect to be nannying all their lives. They certainly love children and are generally domestic types but they are often highly sociable and once they are off-duty many love to hit the local hot spots and boogie the night away. However, unless their night-time activities stop them doing their job properly or, if living-in, they disturb your homelife, you don't need to worry about their nocturnal activities.

What is important is that the nanny fits into *your* idea of what childcare and a good homelife should be. Generally good nannies need to love children, be kind, honest, reliable, flexible and organised and it helps if they have imagination, stamina, initiative and patience too. Just how disciplined, quiet or confident they need to be depends on you and your lifestyle. You will have to decide what she's like from her references and gain your impression of her at the interview. Nobody but you can know if she will fit in with your family's lifestyle - and even you may be unsure.

It is worth thinking through what kind of person you would like to have before you interview candidates. Would you like a quiet home-loving type who stays in her room watching T.V. on her nights off or would you like a bubbly, sociable type who loves meeting your friends and spends many nights out at clubs and bars? Would you like someone very English who understands your way of life or a down-to-earth Aussie or Kiwi who gets on with the job and won't take any nonsense? Nannying is such a personal business that the character and lifestyle of the nanny are as important as her qualifications and experience.

CHAPTER 4

DAY-TO-DAY LIFE WITH A NANNY

"You know your children are wild if the nanny arrives for work in combat gear"
Jasmine Birtles

It can take a few months for a nanny or any other regular child-carer to settle in to a family's way of life. Ideally, on her first day you should give her a written list of duties, rules and notes about the children, the house and what you expect from her. For the first couple of weeks at least one parent should be contactable in case she has problems or questions.

A good nanny will set up her own routine for the children very quickly but even the best nanny will take a few days to adapt to your family's needs.

EMPLOYER/EMPLOYEE RELATIONSHIP

Oh it was all so simple in the olden days wasn't it? You had your Upstairs and you had your Downstairs and never the twain would meet (except occasionally in the young master's bedroom perhaps). Nowadays class consciousness is frowned upon and many nannies, quite rightly, feel very annoyed if they are treated as 'servants'. The fact is, though, that you are the boss, you pay the wages and ultimately what you say goes. So how do you maintain a balanced, harmonious relationship with your nanny while getting what you want out of her?

Respect, kindness and flexibility are the three most important qualities that *both* sides need to express. Set your ground rules from the start. If you would feel most comfortable being called Mrs or Mr X rather than by your Christian name make that clear to the nanny. If she won't accept that then she is not the nanny for you. Both sides should respect the other's privacy and neither should encroach upon the other.

The nanny needs to know which parts of the house, if any, are out-of bounds at any time and if there are any objects that she must not use. Again, give her clear instructions on these *from the start*. Another important subject is guests: if she 'lives in' can she have friends staying with her overnight (female or male)? Can she give dinner parties? Can she have other nannies and their charges to tea? If she is your first nanny you might not know at once how you will feel about any of these things but do your best to make rules at the beginning and then try and break it to her gently if things are not right.

Some parents insist on their nanny being home before a certain time at night. This is entirely up to you but be warned that many nannies love to socialize and feel they can cope perfectly well if they come home at 2 a.m. and have to start work again at 7. These girls would not stay in a job that restricted their nocturnal activities. On the other hand, it can be very disruptive to the family routine if you never know when she'll come home at night - or indeed *if* she'll come home. Imposing a curfew on working days only could be a happy compromise. Ultimately, though, you have to decide what you can put up with and what you can't and then stick to it.

SMOKING

The vast majority of employers prefer non-smoking nannies and if you are very much against the 'vile weed' being anywhere near your children you are quite within your rights to insist that if she must smoke she only does so outside the house when she is off-duty. Even if you do not object to cigarettes yourself it is worth considering the health and safety risks of someone smoking in your home together with the increased risk of the nanny becoming ill or not having enough breath to run after the children.

DRINKING

Some nannies do some nannies don't much but whatever her tastes you should not expect a nanny to be drinking on the job. Drunkenness on duty is a sackable offence in nannying but thankfully it is pretty rare. Rather less rare are drunken nights on the town followed by monster hangovers the next morning.

As a general rule it is reasonable to expect nannies to be fit and able to work when they are on duty so if their late-night drinking affects their work this can jeopardise their job. A nanny needs to be told immediately if this behaviour is unacceptable to you and if it continues after two or three warnings you can quite reasonably sack her. But remember, it cuts both ways. Drunken employers can be impossible to deal with and if you become an 'antisocial' drinker you may find that the nanny is out of the door faster than you can say "hold the tonic"!

SEX AND BOYFRIENDS

Possibly one of the thorniest issues of modern nannying!

Nannies have boyfriends; it's a simple fact of life and sometimes this can be a blessing. If your nanny is from far away, or even just from the next town, having a boyfriend nearby can make her stay much longer than she would otherwise. But others who suddenly discover men can turn from reliable, highly-trained workers into hormonal, doe-eyed, moody drips overnight.

It's a difficult subject to cover with a new nanny but unless you are very liberal you will probably not want to have boyfriends staying overnight, particularly as the nanny often sleeps very close to the children. This is generally accepted by live-in nannies and they know that on the whole boyfriends have to stay away from family life. This is also the reason why so many older nannies want to live out.

THE CAR

More and more parents need nannies who can drive but surprisingly there are still many nannies who have not yet learnt to drive. However, for those who can drive, the use of the family car or, even better, having their own car, is seen as a perk. In fact, really top nannies not only insist on having a car but will only accept certain makes!

If you do provide her with her own car you, or the nanny, will have to pay tax on it (see page 76) and of course you will have to have her insured. This can be particularly hurtful to your purse if she is under 25 and does not have a no-claims bonus. You should explain to her how expensive it could be to you both if she had an accident in the car. In fact it would be useful to decide between you at the beginning who will pay for any repairs not covered by the insurance. Nannies do have accidents sometimes so you should both be prepared.

Safety is of paramount importance. You should check that the nanny has a clean driving licence and, as part of your interview of a prospective nanny, it is important to give the nanny a quick driving test. You might even need to give her a few driving lessons - particularly if she is from abroad. Once you take her on you should make sure she knows that the children should have their seat-belts on at all times and should only be in the back seat.

THE PHONE

The telephone can be such a contentious issue that many parents find that it's worth installing a separate line for the nanny or even buying her a mobile phone. Many young nannies genuinely have no idea how much phone calls are because they have never had to pay the phone bill. If they don't have separate lines it is worth joining Mercury for long-distance and foreign calls as they have a separate billing system where everyone has their own code to punch in before the number. Of course BT offers itemized phone bills too so some of the local calls can be checked but in general, if you do not have a separate line you will need to remind her gently that long phone calls cost you money and she should keep them brief.

Now that mobile phones are so cheap to buy you might consider an Orange or Mercury One to One as viable alternatives. After all, if she had a mobile with her you could contact her at any time and if there were an emergency with the children when they were out of the house she would be able to call for help immediately. Worth looking into!

DRESS

Some people like their nanny to wear a uniform - particularly if she is a Norland, Chiltern or Princess Christian nanny who all have their own uniforms - but most prefer their girls to look smart but casual. Some nannies *like* to wear a uniform because it saves their own clothes, makes them feel more professional and is a visible sign that they are on duty as opposed to the time when they are wearing their own things and therefore off-duty.

If you both decide that she should wear her own clothes make it clear to her from the beginning how you want her to look - if you have an opinion on that.

CONFIDENTIALITY

In the sample contract we have printed on page 45 you will see that we have included a clause on confidentiality. It goes without saying that an employee should respect your privacy and not gossip to all and sundry about how you behave in your home.

Of course it's a fact of life that nannies, like any other human beings, do gossip and there's not much you can do about it, but if she has signed that contract and then starts to spread stories about you that actually cause you problems then you can, if necessary, resort to the courts. It's worse if you're famous or in an important position. Sara Netanyahu, wife of the Israeli president, suffered at the hands of the tabloids when she sacked her nanny for burning some soup. The disgruntled girl told all to the press before anyone could stop her. TV presenter Anne Diamond had to get a court injunction to stop newspapers printing a story from a former nanny who had worked for her for just seven weeks.

Hopefully you will not have to go to such drastic lengths but, equally, you may find it wise to keep important things private even if you think the nanny is a complete angel. She is still a paid employee and not really one of the family. You can't be too careful.

HOME LIFE GENERALLY

Respect on both sides is the key to a successful working partnership with your nanny. When you are living and working in the same confined area it's often the little, petty things that can break up a happy relationship. You will both need to set boundaries - geographical, social and work-related - so that you both know where you stand. She should make it clear what she is not prepared to do and the maximum number of hours she is prepared to work.

You should make it clear where she is allowed to go, what aspects of your social life she is welcome to join and what she is and is not allowed to do with the children.

You should not be embarrassed about your preferences for modes of behaviour in your home. For example, nannies should be accepted as part of the family but if you prefer to eat on your own she should be told that at the beginning. She herself might prefer the peace and quiet of eating on her own, in which case she should be allowed that privilege.

It is very much a question of give and take but if you have chosen wisely you will find that you will only gain if you give a little more than you might otherwise - both in money and in concessions - and you will keep your nanny for much longer.

CHAPTER 5

THE CONTRACT

"An oral contract is not worth the paper it's written on."
Sam Goldwyn.

It may seem ridiculously formal but in many cases a properly-written contract signed by both parties can save a lot of heartache and bad feeling later on. If the duties and hours that the nanny will work are actually written down then everyone knows where they stand. Also it gives you more clout if she is clearly shirking or is persistently late for work.

Most agencies have a basic contract that they will draw up for individual families - we certainly do - but if you would like to write your own here is a sample one for you to use:

NANNY CONTRACT OF EMPLOYMENT

This contract is subject to the laws governing Great Britain and Ireland.

Date of Issue......................

Name and address of employer:

Name and address of employee:

Date of commencement of employment................
Previous service (if any) counting towards continuous employment:
Job title:

REMUNERATION

The salary is...................per week*/month* before/after the deduction of Tax and National Insurance payable monthly.

The employer will ensure that the employer's and employee's National Insurance Contributions and Income Tax are paid.

HOURS OF WORK

Days/hours to be worked, including baby-sitting requirements (if appropriate) will be agreed by the employer and employee in advance and will be:

These hours of work can only be changed by mutual agreement.

DUTIES

Child/Children's names and ages:

Duties:

The employee shall be entitled to:
  Accommodation*
  Bathroom: sole use/shared*
  Meals*
  Use of car on duty/off duty*. (Petrol costs will be reimbursed at the rate recommended by the AA if the employee uses his/her own car.)

HOLIDAYS

The employee will be allowed.............weeks paid holiday in each year. In the first or final year of service the employee will be entitled to holidays on a pro rata basis.

Paid compensation is not normally given for holidays not actually taken. Holidays may only be carried into the next year with the express permission of the employer.

The employee will be free on all Bank Holidays or will receive a day off in lieu, by agreement.

SICKNESS

The employer will pay SSP scheme in accordance with legislation*. Any additional sick pay will be at the employer's discretion (or insert details of additional sick pay scheme).

TERMINATION

In the first four weeks of employment, one week's notice is required on either side. After four weeks' continuous service, either the employee or the employer may terminate this contract by giving..................weeks' notice.

ACCIDENTS

The employee must report all accidents during working hours and while on the employer's premises.

SECURITY

The employee is expected to treat as secret and confidential all knowledge of the Employer's affairs. The employee may not divulge any of the employer's trade secrets or confidential information to a third party either during their employment or at any time thereafter or use any such secrets or information for any purpose other than those authorised by and for the employer. As a condition of employment she/he must execute prior to or on the date of commencement of employment and from time to time such undertakings as to confidentiality, trade secrets and inventions as the employer may require.

PENSIONS

The employer does/does not* run a pension scheme.

DISCIPLINE

Reasons which might give rise to the need for disciplinary measures include the following:
1. Causing a disruptive influence in the household.
2. Job incompetence.
3. Unsatisfactory standard of dress or appearance.
4. Conduct during or outside working hours prejudicial to the interest or reputation of the employer.
5. Unreliability in time-keeping or attendance.

6. Failure to comply with instructions and procedures, e.g. being unable to drive due to driving ban.
7. Breach of confidentiality clause.

In the event of the need to take disciplinary action the procedure will be:

First   -   Oral warning
Second   -   Written warning
Third   -   Dismissal

Reasons which might give rise to summary dismissal include the following:
1. Theft
2. Drunkenness
3. Illegal drug taking
4. Child abuse

Behaviour of employer unacceptable to the employee include:
1. Sexual harassment
2. Drunkenness
3. Illegal drug taking

Signed by the employer..

Signed by the employee..

(*delete as appropriate)

CHAPTER 6

MALE NANNIES

*"It's not the men in my life
it's the life in my men."*
Mae West.

In these times of equality of the sexes it is quite reasonable that some men should want to become nannies. Many are gentle and caring and make superb childcarers. There are a few male NNEBs and most of them get jobs in state-run nurseries. A small percentage get jobs in families, usually ones where most of the children are boys.

Equally, though, there are some thoroughly undesirable men who want to go into child 'care' for very much the wrong reasons. One can say the same for some women, but the percentage is much lower in girls than in boys who want to work with children. We have occasionally had male applicants - nannies and au pairs - and have placed a few but we have also rejected a number because we were just not sure of them. We have never had any definite cause for alarm but it seems best to err on the side of caution.

It will take a long time for employers in this country to get used to the idea of a male nanny but if you do consider it you will feel more secure if you interview him thoroughly, grill his referees and, if you take him on, tell your children to let you know if they are at all unhappy with him.

CHAPTER 7

AU PAIRS

"She's a very quiet girl and she likes quiet things, like the folding of money."
Bob Monkhouse.

If you're appalled at the cost of a full-time nanny you may be wondering if you could get by with an au pair. If you have babies or very young children we're sorry but the answer is a very emphatic 'no'! With these vulnerable little ones you need someone responsible and experienced who could cope with any emergency. In recent years far too many parents have brought in an au pair to do a nanny's or mother's help's job which has placed an unfair burden on numbers of young women, and men, and has put many children at risk.

However, if you or your partner are at home all day or if you have older children who spend a lot of time at school then an au pair can be an excellent solution. Remember, though, au pairs are generally untrained, inexperienced and are not over here to do a proper job. They are young people who want to learn English and find out about the British way of life first and foremost which is why they usually take language classes while they are here. In return for some *light* housework and childminding they expect a room and board, some pocket money and a welcome into an English family.

WHO CAN BE AN AU PAIR?

According to the Home Office an au pair should be a single person between the ages of 17 and 27 inclusive. They must either come from one of the EEC countries (such as France, Germany, Spain or Italy) or they can come from one of the following countries:

- **Andorra**
- **Bosnia-Herzegovina**
- **Croatia**
- **Cyprus**
- **Czech Republic**
- **Faroe Islands**
- **Greenland**
- **Hungary**
- **Liechtenstein**
- **Macedonia**
- **Malta**
- **Monaco**
- **San Marino**
- **Slovak Republic**
- **Slovenia**
- **Switzerland**

There is also a provision for Commonwealth girls and boys to do something like an au pair job here. So long as they are aged 17 to 27 they can enter the country on the Holidaymaker scheme which allows them to stay in the UK up to two years on the condition that they have sufficient funds to return home and want to do some paid work. Usually this means that Australian, New Zealand, Canadian or South African women or men work as nannies or mother's helps but if they're very young and inexperienced and have enough money to keep themselves in clothes and drinks at the bar they might look for an au pair position instead.

You will generally find that most au pairs, other than those from EEC countries, come from Croatia, Czech Republic, Hungary, Malta, Slovak Republic, Slovenia and Turkey.

If you are bringing in an au pair from abroad (rather than taking one that is already in Britain) you may need to know that au pairs from Bosnia-Herzegovina, Macedonia and Turkey are required by the Home Office to obtain a visa before travelling to this country.

Non-EEC au pairs also have to register with the police as soon as they arrive if they have been allowed to stay here for longer than six months. They have to take their passport and two passport-sized photographs to their local police station and will have to pay an Alien's Registration Fee.

THE MALE AU PAIR

After the celebrated case a few years ago in which a Swedish boy went to court to win the right to be an au pair, boys from several countries - particularly the former Eastern block - have been pestering agencies to find them work. Naturally many parents are wary about leaving their children with a boy or man they do not know, but, as with male nannies, there have been some very successful placements particularly in families that have boys.

A good male au pair can be a wonderful addition to a family, especially if the father is absent. He can become a surrogate brother, to the children and provide a positive role model for the boys - something that is sadly lacking in so many communities around the country now. Many are very handy around the house and can be relied upon to change plugs, mend the car or even do bits of DIY. They can kick a ball around and are sometimes better at coping with boisterous children than their female counterparts. Many of the male au pairs from Eastern Europe are qualified, or nearly qualified, in medicine, engineering or one of the other professions and simply want to improve their English in order to help their careers, so some can be particularly mature.

Of course, as in any of the caring professions, there are some unsavoury characters who want to get into childcare for the wrong reasons. We have been approached by a *few* men that we rejected. However, we have placed a number of male au pairs who have been so successful that their families didn't want them to leave and asked them to come back when they could.

If you are tempted by the idea of a male au pair you should trust your gut feeling when you interview him. It helps if he is in this country already so that you can meet him face-to-face but if you talk to him over the phone ask him questions about his former experience in childcare. Also check his references very thoroughly.

HOW DO I FIND A GOOD AU PAIR?

By contacting us, of course! No seriously, there are many ways of obtaining an au pair but by far the quickest and safest is through an agency. Certainly if you have friends abroad who have a daughter or a friend who would like to come here as an au pair that is often a cheap and fairly safe way to go about it. There is the danger that you will fall out with the au pair and therefore with your friends abroad but you may feel this is a risk you are prepared to take.

Generally if you want to be really safe it is worth paying money to a reputable agency (and remember there are some disreputable ones) who will often have contacts abroad who provide them with good people and who check references of all the girls and boys before they send them out.

You should interview a prospective au pair either face-to-face, if they are in the country, or on the phone at home. It would be useful to ask him/her questions about their experience of childcare and if she/he is prepared to help with the housework. Here are some questions you may find helpful:

1. Can you cook? What kind of food do you cook?

2. Do you have lots of ideas for entertaining the children? What are they?

3. Do you smoke?

4. Do you have any special dietary needs

5. (If you have pets) Do you get on with animals? Are you allergic to them?

6. Are you happy to help with household chores?

7. Will you do some babysitting?

8. Do you want to take language classes? If so, have you found a course or would you like help finding one?

If you pick an au pair who is still in her home country you may have to write a letter of invitation to her so that she can obtain a visa. This is not necessary with au pairs from European Union countries.

WHAT CAN AN AU PAIR DO?

Again, the Home Office rules are quite clear about the amount of work an au pair can do. They are only allowed to work a *maximum* of five hours a day for a *maximum* of five days a week and they should have a full two days off per week. Quite often they are expected to do one or two evenings babysitting per week but this is not specified in the Home Office's rules. Also, according to their rules, au pairs may only do that 'job' for up to two years. However, many au pairs only want to be here for six months so that ruling will probably not apply to you anyway.

You may have heard the term 'au pair plus'. This is not a proper au pair job as far as the Home Office is concerned and, although a number of agencies provide girls for 'au pair plus' jobs, we are usually unhappy about it.

The idea of au pair plus is that an au pair works more than the statutory 25 hours a week and is therefore paid more. This type of au pair might do 40 hours and be paid £60 a week which is considerably cheaper than a live-in nanny who would expect at least £100 for that. But we sometimes find that what is described as 'au pair plus' is often little more than slavery!

Most EU girls are not interested in this kind of work. Girls (and boys) from Eastern Europe will often grab the job, even though they are not legally allowed to, in the hope that it will mean they can stay here and have more money to spend. Even these girls and boys, though, will leave in tears or disgust after a while if they find they are being used and abused. You may be lucky and find someone who has a lot of experience of childcare, on whom you can rely and trust with your children and your possessions but you are always taking more of a risk when you give an au pair responsibility than when you give it to a proper nanny.

DO'S AND DON'TS WITH AU PAIRS

Au pairs tend to be the most exploited of all the childcarers and although there are many parents who are delightful to their au pairs and genuinely treat them as part of the family, there is also a depressingly large number that sees these foreign visitors as slave labour. It is usually these employers who are stunned to find that their au pair has done 'a runner' during the night or that girl after girl suddenly announces that her grandmother/uncle/first-cousin-once-removed is seriously ill/dying/dead and she has to rush back home to be with the loved one.

That excuse, by the way, is the oldest in the book and if your au pair throws it at you it's time to sit her or him down and ask what the problem really is.

So here is a list of big do's and big don'ts if you want to hire, and keep, an au pair:

DO

- ... make sure they have a pleasant, clean room that is their own private space. The linen on their bed should be clean (we have come across parents who didn't provide clean sheets!) and the room should not be used by any other member of the family or be used to store their belongings.

- ... allow them to eat whatever the family is eating or, if they have particular dietary requirements, (for moral, religious or health reasons) you should provide them with food that is acceptable to them.

- ... treat them as part of the family and take them on outings and trips that the family goes on.

- ... pay them a reasonable amount. The Home Office guidelines say they should be paid a minimum of £35 a week but we find that au pairs are much more likely to stay and are more willing to help if they are paid around £45 a week basic.

- ... find out about local colleges where the au pair can learn the language.

DON'T

- ... treat them like servants. Not only will they become sullen or clumsy due to fear but they will probably not last very long.

- ... treat them like a stranger. They have come here to be part of the family so make sure you care for them as if they were a niece or nephew.

BEWARE!

Many au pairs from the former Eastern block try to move from being au pairs to becoming mother's helps or nannies. They offer their services at cut-down prices because they know they would be working illegally but are so anxious to stay they will work for very little. Of course it is very tempting to take them on as proper English or antipodean nannies can be pricey but there are many reasons why you should not:

- It is illegal and you personally could be prosecuted for knowingly employing an illegal immigrant. As this book goes to press the Government is introducing even tougher measures to stop people working here who should not be working.

- Illegal workers are very vulnerable and it would be easy to treat them as slaves.

- These girls (and boys) are very rarely experienced enough to take sole charge of a child and it's even more rare that they have any childcare qualifications. You could be putting your children and your home at risk by leaving her, or him, unsupervised.

CHAPTER 8

MATERNITY NURSES

*"When I had my baby I screamed and screamed.
And that was just the conception."
Joan Rivers.*

DO I NEED A MATERNITY NURSE?

That depends on what you are like, how your health is, how much money you have and whether this is your first child or not. Some mothers swear by maternity nurses and in some cases keep them on for years. Others either could not afford one anyway (they are expensive) or would not want someone else to look after their new precious bundle.

Maternity nurses, who are basically experienced and well-trained nannies who have a particular passion for babies, can be very useful if you are a new mother. They can give you a crash course in how to give your baby the very best care, get the baby into a routine, and will make the recovery period much shorter by giving you the chance to rest as much as you need. Working mothers who want to be back in the office as soon as possible after the birth find them invaluable.

If you have had a particularly difficult birth and you do not have a relative to look after things while you recuperate, a maternity nurse will make all the difference. She can look after all the baby's needs, bring it to you to be breast-fed if that is what you are doing and then take it away until the next feed. She can take care of all the changing, the burping, the washing and the sleepless nights; getting up when the baby cries. If you are the sort of person who is happy with a rather more 'hands-off' experience with your new-born then a maternity nurse will be a great treat. It is up to you how long you have her for; a month or two is the norm but you may all get on so well that she stays for longer.

On the other hand, new mother or not, you may find that you would prefer to have someone in to do the housework, cooking and all the day-to-day chores of running a home while you concentrate entirely on looking after baby. In that case it would be useful to contact an agent either for a temporary housekeeper or a mother's help who is willing do more housework than childcaring.

HOW DO I GET ONE?

...by booking her early. New parents are often shocked at how quickly they have to book a maternity nurse. Demand for them outstrips supply even more than with nannies and you will often find that maternity nurses are booked up for at least the next nine months. The moment you have decided that you would like to have one, start looking.

You may be lucky enough to have one recommended by a friend, ring her up and find that she is free. Well done if that happens to you! Otherwise it is best to contact an agency. There are a couple that specialize in maternity nurses but most nanny agencies have some on their books.

Maternity nurses are self-employed and therefore pay their own tax and National Insurance but they still command a slightly higher salary than most nannies. It's unlikely that you will find one for less than £250 a week - at least, not one that it is worth having! The average is £60 per day. In London you could pay up to £500 a week for a really good one. Maternity nurses who specialize in caring for twins are particularly highly paid, but then they need to be!

As with nannies, it is imperative that you interview any prospective maternity nurse thoroughly and check her references. At the interview ask her questions such as the following:

1. What are your qualifications (ask to see certificates)?

2. How many years' experience have you had?

3. How long would you be prepared to stay?

4. Why did you become a maternity nurse?

5. Do you mind disposable nappies?

6. Do you smoke?

7. What are your ideas on feeding babies? Are you in favour of demand feeding or getting the baby into a feeding routine?

8. Are you in favour of breast-feeding?

9. (If you have children already) Do you mind the other children being around the baby during the day?

Show the nurse where she will be sleeping and check on her own dietary needs. She will probably also guide you on the kinds of clothes, equipment, foodstuffs and toys you should be buying now to prepare for the new arrival.

Again, trust your judgement when you interview applicants. Although it is true that maternity nurses are relatively rare it would be terrible to have someone in the house 24 hours a day that you just could not stand. Some can be bossy, though well-meaning, so you will have to decide if you can cope with this. Others may have definite views on the rearing of children that are quite opposite to yours so that would never work. You will know, at the interview, if you ask enough searching questions (and please don't be embarrassed; this is your one big chance!) whether you can live with this person for a month or more. You will also get a good idea of her personality and ability from her referees so make sure you ask them a lot of questions too.

WHAT TO EXPECT FROM A MATERNITY NURSE

You will have booked your maternity nurse for the day on which you expect your baby to be born but, babies being what they are, you may have to wait for days or weeks after that date for the baby itself actually to decide to come out and see the world. If the maternity nurse is ready and waiting to work with you you should be prepared to pay her for being on standby. We recommend that you pay her half pay for the first week and full pay for any weeks after that. If she just has to wait for a few days she may waive payment but you should be prepared to pay her half rate for those few days if necessary.

Maternity nurses are on duty 24 hours a day (hence the high pay) and once she has been with you for a week she should have at least 24 hours off per week. A good one will not only care for your baby but will show you how to look after it properly. She will teach you how to feed, wash, dress and exercise the little one and will give you a good daily routine to follow. She will give you advice on a suitable diet for breast-feeding mothers and, if you have had complications in the birth, give you some basic nursing.

Maternity nurses should be treated as part of the family. Yours may prefer to eat alone but generally she should be invited to eat with you and, if she does not have her own sitting room, to rest and relax with the family. Just to be on the safe side it is worth drawing up a contract of employment with the nurse when you take her on. It may seem excessive for such a short term of employment but it often avoids nastiness if things aren't done in the way you agreed at the interview.

CHAPTER 9

WHY USE AN AGENCY?

"Scientists have just discovered something that can do the work of ten men - a woman."
anon

Good question. After all, agencies come in all shapes and sizes and at various levels of competence. Why bother and are they worth their fee?

It depends on the agency. There are many of them around the country. Some specialise in nannies or in au pairs or in domestic workers. Others offer some of everything. Nanny agencies often only last for a year or two because the people who set them up don't realise how difficult and expensive they are to run. It's worth asking an agency how long they have been in business when you call them. If they have lasted longer than two years you can be fairly sure that they will last long enough to give you compensation if anything should go wrong with your nanny.

When you contact an agency they should send you a copy of their terms and conditions of business which usually look boring but should be read. Here you will find out how long their guarantee period is, what your obligations are and what you can reasonably expect the agency to do.

Since 1995 it has not been necessary for agencies to obtain a license to operate. This means that absolutely anyone can set up any sort of agency and you have no way of knowing what their background is. Therefore, it helps if you know someone who has had a good experience with an agency so that you can follow their recommendation.

Another safeguard for parents is the agency's membership of the Federation of Recruitment and Employment Services (FRES). Employment agencies can become full members of FRES after they have been trading for at least two years. If you have a big complaint against an agency that belongs to the Federation you can contact them on 0171.323.4300 and might be able to have the agency struck off their list. In fact if you have a particularly strong complaint you can also report them to:

>   The Employment Agency Standards Office
>   Exchange House
>   Exchange Road
>   Watford
>   Herts
>   WD1 7HH
>   (01923.210706)

WHAT DOES AN AGENCY DO?

An agency's business is finding good nannies and other childcarers from all over the country - and the world - and matching them with the needs of their clients. It is not an easy job and involves a good deal of advertising, travelling round the country to talk to students taking nannying courses, endless interviews, checking of references and qualifications and dealing with problems before and after a nanny has started work. The day-to-day running of an agency involves very long hours (if it's done properly) constant phonecalls all around the world and the ability to deal with a wide range of personalities and problems.

Using a good agency (and there are bad ones, beware!) should save you all the hassle and worry of advertising, sifting through calls from highly unsuitable people and interviewing people cold. Good agencies are constantly meeting nannies, mother's helps and au pairs and will reject some that they think are not good enough for their clients. Those agencies will sometimes reject clients, too, if they will not offer a proper salary for the hours and duties they are demanding, or if the client has needs that the agency knows they will not be able to meet. Again, a good agency will have connections with other, similar agencies (perhaps through FRES) and can put these clients onto one of those if they think the other agency could help them.

Good agencies will guarantee a nanny for a certain period after she/he has started work. If she/he leaves precipitously, through no fault of yours, or becomes thoroughly unsuitable, they will either replace her or return to you a portion of the fee you paid them. You can ask agencies for their Scale of Rebate when you first phone them up if you want to be sure.

However, if a nanny leaves because the employer reneges on the original agreement, perhaps by trying to pay her less than was agreed or piling on duties or hours that she hadn't been told of at the start, then they will have forfeited any right to repayment by the agency.

Nannying works only when there is respect on all sides. Good agencies respect their nannies as well as their clients and will try to be even-handed in their dealings with both. As we said before, there are good and bad nannies as well as good and bad clients and a proper agency will hear the grievances of both before deciding what action to take.

If you or the nanny experience problems in your working relationship a good agency will mediate and, if necessary, explain to one or both of you how your behaviour should be changed to bring back harmony. A really good agency (like us of course) will step in and try to help however long the nanny has been with you.

Agencies can also help you set up a contract, advise you on a reasonable salary for the hours and duties you want and tell you where to find out about tax and National Insurance payments for your nanny.

HOW TO GET THE MOST OUT OF AN AGENCY

Good agencies will ask you a lot of questions and it helps if you have thought through your needs, your likes, your dislikes and the fundamentals of the job (salary, hours, duties etc) before you phone. If you don't like the sound of the voice on the other end of the phone, or are put off by their attitude, don't bother with them.

When describing the job to the agency be as honest and complete in your description of the job, your home and the children as possible. Let them know if one or more of your children is particularly difficult or has problems; don't make the nanny's room or your home sound better than they are, and don't try and make out that it is an easy, light job if it isn't. You will waste your time as much as anyone else's when the agency sends you nannies who are interested in a job that is quite different from the reality.

If the agency is new to you and you want to check that it is bona fide don't be afraid of asking them questions such as:

- What are their charges?

- What is their guarantee period?

- What aftercare do they provide and how long for?

- Do they interview all the nannies they send out for jobs?

- Do they check references themselves and if so how many and do they do it by phone or letter or both?

- Where do they get their nannies from?

- Are they a member of FRES? Do they have a licence?

SAFETY

If you have hired a nanny or other childcarer through an agency you have a much better chance of finding someone trustworthy than if you went through the whole process on your own. Agencies have to sift through some very unsuitable types to find the good workers which you would have to do on your own if you advertised privately.

Agencies that belong to FRES give each other information on bad nannies which helps them reject girls that might seem to be perfectly good. This is something else the private employer does not have.

Also, the simple fact of two lots of people rather than one interviewing someone and checking their references cuts down the chances of bad nannies slipping through the net into your home.

IS IT JUST LUCK?

Sometimes, yes. Some families seem to be lucky in the nannies who have fallen into their laps and they are surprised, but grateful, that they found her. But more often it is parents' determination to interview a number of nannies, ask them searching questions and grill their referees that helps them find the perfect nanny.

Some parents are unlucky in their choice of nanny once or twice, but families who keep having bad experiences with childcarers may find that there is something wrong with their attitude or their treatment of these employees that causes such problems. We discuss this further on page 74.

FRES

If you have no idea where to go to choose the right agency you will be safest if you contact FRES direct and ask them for their list of nanny agencies. They are always pleased to help and will also give you information on how best to use an agency (you can find their phone number on page 88).

CHAPTER 10

DON'T!

"Truce is stranger than friction."
Bob Monkhouse.

As an agency we are always wary of parents who say that all their nannies have left after a few months. They could have been unlucky and had a couple of nannies who happened to be unsuitable or had to move on for personal reasons but if three or more nannies in succession up and leave then there is something wrong with the family.

There are a few reasons why some families go through a string of unsuccessful nannies. Some parents try and pretend at the interview that the job is something it isn't or they'll promise a certain salary and then actually pay less per week or even try to get out of paying at all! Some parents - often without realising it - will exploit the nanny by loading extra little duties on her each day or coming home hours late without warning and not giving her time off in lieu or, if she's living in, by expecting her to get up with the baby every night after she has worked a ten-hour day. Others are plain neurotic and expect complete perfection with everything spotless and doused in bleach at all times.

Of course if you are losing nannies regularly it may be because you have not yet learnt to interview thoroughly enough so you keep picking the wrong ones or it may be that in your heart of hearts you don't really want to have someone else looking after your child so you keep choosing unsuitable people. Whatever it is, if you find that your front entrance has become a revolving door for nannies you should take a good look at your life and your attitude to childcare and do something about it before the children are even more unsettled by the quick turnover. As we have said before, successful nannying depends on respect and flexibility on both sides. Ask yourself, do I respect my nanny and the job that she/he does? If you honestly answer 'no' to that question then you should rethink the whole issue.

CHAPTER 11

NANNY TAX AND NATIONAL INSURANCE

(Don't skip this - it's important)

"We were so poor when I was a kid all we had to wear were hand-me-downs, which was tough on me since I was an only child." Gene Peret.

Ugh! Tax; National Insurance; those dreaded words! As if you weren't paying enough each week to keep the girl you have to pay yet more for her tax and National Insurance. And yes, you *do*, have to pay it. Your nanny is an employee like anyone else and has a right to having her tax and her national insurance contributions paid by her employer: you.

There are certainly people who try to avoid paying. Some say that their nanny earns less than £61 a week - below the tax and National Insurance threshold - and then they top her salary up with cash. But there are problems with this practice:

- It is illegal under tax legislation.
- The nanny will not earn any rights to a pension or employment benefits.
- When the Revenue catches up with you you will be liable to pay all the tax and NI including interest and penalties. You have no legal right to make the nanny pay it.

Another little wheeze some people try is to say that their nanny is self-employed. But in fact, even if she is part-time or in a nanny-share scheme the tax office still regards her as an employee because:

- You can decide what hours she will work and for what rates of pay.
- She does not provide her own equipment and materials.
- The nanny is not able to hire other people to do the work instead of her.

Some people choose antipodean nannies on the assumption that they won't have to pay tax and NI for them. This again is not true. No foreign worker is exempted from paying tax and National Insurance. However, a lot of people get away with not paying foreign girls' tax and contributions because they are often not in the country long enough for the taxman to realise they are earning anything.

By the way, make sure you and the nanny are clear from the start whether the salary you are offering is gross or net. Nannies tend to think in terms of net pay so you may have to tell her the salary in those terms too. But do let her know what the gross pay is and what the gross annual salary will be too so that she is reminded that you will be paying her tax and National Insurance.

If you have looked at the chart on page 7 to show how much a nanny will cost you, gross, per week and it all looks too complex, you could contact one of the various companies who offer a nanny-tax service (see ad on page 95).

DIY TAX

Once you have found your nanny (lucky you!) you must inform your local Inland Revenue tax office and they will send you an information pack. The information from the Revenue office will show you how to calculate the tax and N.I. which is deducted from the nanny's gross pay. Of course, most nannies negotiate their net pay so you may need to ask your tax office to calculate the necessary gross pay for you. You are also required to provide your nanny with weekly/monthly payslips showing clearly that deductions have been made.

You should keep a record of the gross and net pay, tax and N.I. on a form sent to you by the Revenue. Then at the end of each tax year, you will be sent, and be required to complete, a form summarising the amounts for the year. It helps if you can send the tax office your nanny's P45 which her last employer should have given her on leaving.

Just to add to your joys, you may need to pay tax on any perk the nanny has such as a car and petrol. The Revenue will send you a form P11D at the end of each year on which you should itemize these extras. Technically the tax on these items is the nanny's liability but if you have agreed a net pay with her she will expect you to pay the tax.

N.B. As an agency we believe that parents who are conscientious about paying tax and National Insurance for their nannies are likely to be good employers who will keep their nannies for a long time. We find the same thing with our agency fee. Parents who try to get out of paying that are usually the ones who try to pay their nanny less than they originally stated or try to make her work longer hours than she should. It is all about fair play and consideration for the work and lives of others. Paying your nanny's contributions ensures that she is helped in sickness and old age which is what she deserves.

SICK PAY

A full-time nanny or mother's help should expect up to four weeks' full pay per year while she is sick. It is a good idea to include the sick pay details in the original contract (see page 45 for our sample contract).

Full-time nannies are eligible for Statutory Sick Pay (SSP) in certain circumstances, and it can go some way to making up a nanny's salary while she's ill. Your nanny can only become eligible for SSP after four consecutive days of absence from work. If your nanny is well-paid you may find that the SSP is relatively small so her illness will still cost you quite a lot - particularly if you have to bring in temporary help.

SSP is earnings related so, when you take on a nanny, contact your local DHSS office to find out the current rate. SSP is treated as pay by the Inland Revenue so you will have to deduct tax and NI contributions from it and give it to the nanny net in the normal way.

The DHSS or your local tax office will send you information on how to work out if you can claim back some SSP on the money you have paid your sick nanny and if so how to do it. It is rather complicated but basically you have to work out the total gross Class 1 national Insurance liability for that tax month in which she was ill. Multiply that figure by 13 per cent (round up to fractions of a penny) and then work out the total SSP payments in that month. If the amount of SSP paid is more than 13 per cent of the NIC's due then you can claim back the difference. There, told you it was complicated!

Please don't avoid the issue of sick pay. Nannies are human and can fall sick or be involved in accidents. It is important to be clear at the start what pay you will give her, how long you will pay for, and what you will do if the illness lasts a long time.

There are no particular rules governing payment of au pairs while they are sick although we would recommend that if she is staying with you for, say, six months and she is sick for a few days or a week that you still pay her for that week. It is bad enough to be ill in a foreign country without losing the small amount of money one was counting on.

In all cases, as in the treatment of nannies and au pairs generally, it is best to be generous with sick pay. It reaps dividends in the long run; in some cases it means there *is* a long run!

THE EASY WAY

If all this seems just too annoying and time-consuming you could use the services of a payroll company. There are some who specialize in sorting out tax for nannies and other domestic staff and many payroll companies will organise the whole thing for you for a small monthly charge (see ad on page 95).

MATERNITY RIGHTS

If you need to know about your nanny's maternity rights it is best to contact the Federation of Recruitment and Employment Services (FRES) at 36-38 Mortimer Street, London W1N 7RB (0171.323.4300).

CHAPTER 12

GET CAMPAIGNING

"Many are called but few are called back."
Sister Mary Tricky.

Did you know that the UK is at the bottom of the European Childcare League? Whilst 65 per cent of working women return to work within a year of having a baby only two per cent of British children under five have access to a full-time state nursery place. There is almost no help at all for parents who want to have their children cared for at home. If this makes you angry then get campaigning with one or more of the organisations listed below!

Working for Childcare is an organisation which exists to promote the development of quality childcare that meets the needs of working parents and their children. It was set up in 1984 as the Workplace Nurseries Campaign by a group of parents angered by the sudden imposition of the Workplace Nurseries tax and the lack of suitable childcare. The tax was finally abolished in 1990. Now the organisation specialises in the needs of working parents and their children by giving advice, lobbying parliament, local authorities, employers and trade unions, researching issues and organising conferences and seminars. The organisation stands for choice in childcare and believes in decent pay for childcare workers. Membership is £10 waged or £5 unwaged.

Parents at Work is a national charity committed to the welfare of children of working parents. It believes that the central role played by parents in bringing up their children should be more highly valued and parents should be enabled to make choices about how they balance work and home. It has local support groups all round the country and offers advice, a Helpline, guidance on childcare problems and guidance on practical solutions for balancing work and home. Their membership rate is £18 or £12 for low-income families.

Childcare Vouchers is connected with the Luncheon Vouchers scheme. The idea is that they sell childcare vouchers to businesses which then give them to their employees to pay childcarers - such as nannies, nurseries, childminders or even relatives. Only a few companies currently operate such a scheme but it is worth asking your boss to look into the possibility of bringing it in.

The Maternity Alliance is a national charity which anyone interested in the issues surrounding maternity can join. It aims to improve the care, health, education and social support given to parents before conception, during pregnancy, childbirth and in the first year of their baby's life. The Alliance gives information and advice to newly pregnant women. They organise conferences, seminars and reports on current maternity issues. They offer training courses for those in contact with pregnant women and new families, such as employers, and they launch national campaigns on major issues affecting parents and babies.

If you want to contact any of these organisations you will find their numbers and addresses on page 88.

CHAPTER 13

ABOUT TOP NOTCH NANNIES

"Listen, everyone is entitled to my opinion."
Madonna.

You were wondering when we'd get to the good part weren't you!

Top Notch Nannies is run by Jean Birtles (look at the back cover for her picture) in Kensington, London. There is also a Top Notch Nannies office in New Zealand.

Jean was a teacher for over 25 years and taught pupils of all ages from 3 to 80 (yes, 80!). She is an expert in dealing with children and gives lectures on parenting and childcare. She has appeared on TV and radio giving advice on all aspects of childcare.

Jean started her business four years ago, calling it Brilliant Babysitters. It was then an adjunct of her new teaching agency called The Teaching Team, but when the babysitting business took off immediately and orders flew in for nannies, au pairs and domestic staff of all kinds she decided to concentrate on that side of the business. Very quickly she changed the name to Top Notch Nannies (and Brilliant Au Pairs) as that described the business far more accurately.

The agency provides full and part-time, permanent and temporary nannies, mother's helps, housekeepers and nanny governesses. It also places au pairs and provides a babysitting service. If you would like to place an order or find out more about the agency just contact us at:

**Top Notch Nannies
22a Campden Grove
London   W8 4JG**

or ring us on:

0171.938.2006

or

0171.938.4742

USEFUL NAMES AND ADDRESSES

The Campaign for Tax Relief and Childcare,
Box 23, London SW1 2SB (0171.834.9619)

CACHE
(Council for Awards in Children's Care and Education),
8 Chequer Street, St Albans, Hertfordshire AL1 3XZ
(01727.847636)

Childcare Vouchers,
50 Vauxhall Bridge Road, London SW1 2RS

Chiltern Nursery Training College,
Peppard Road, Caversham, Reading, Berkshire RG4 8JZ

City & Guilds Customer Services Unit,
(0171.294.2805)

Daniel Nursery Stores,
96-122 Uxbridge Road, Ealing, London W13
(0181.567.6789)

The Federation of Recruitment and Employment Services Ltd (FRES),
36-38 Mortimer Street, London W1N 7RB (0171.323.4300)

The Isle College,
Ramneth Road, Wisbech, Cambridgeshire PE13 2JE

Le Club Tricolore
10 Ballingdon Road, London, SW11 6AJ (0171 924 4649)

The London Montessori Centre,
18 Balderton Street, London W1Y 1TG

Lucy Clayton College of Nursery Training,
4, Cornwall Gardens, London SW7 4AJ (0171.581.0024)

Maternity Alliance,
15 Britannia Street, London SC1X 9JP (0171.588.8582)

Nannytax,
P.O. Box 988, Brighton BN2 1BY (01273.626256)

NAMCW
(The National Association for Maternal and Child Welfare Ltd), First Floor, 40-42 Osnaburgh Street, London NW1 3ND (0171.383.4117)

National Association of Nursery Nurses,
c/o The Wayside, Hurworth on Tees, Darlington, Co. Durham DL2 2EE (01325.720511)

National Childbirth Trust,
Alexandra House, Alton Terrace, London W3 6NH (0181.992.8637)

Norland Nursery Training College,
Denford Park, Hungerford, Berkshire RG17 OPQ

The Princess Christian College,
26 Wilbraham Road, Fallowfield, Manchester M14 6JX

The Professional Association of Nursery Nurses,
2 St James' Court, Friar Gate, Derby DE1 1BT
(01332.343029)

Squidgy Things Ltd
8 Motcomb Street, London SW1X 8JU

Top Notch Nannies,
22a Campden Grove, London W8 4DX
(0171.938.2006/4742)

Working for Childcare,
77 Holloway Road, London N7 8JZ (0171.700.0281)

Working Mother's Association,
77 Holloway Road, London N7 8JZ (0171.700.5771)

RECOMMENDED READING

The Briefcase and the Baby
- A. Cuthbert and A.Holford (Mandarin)

The Good Nanny Guide
- Charlotte Breese and Hilaire Gomer (Vermillion)

The Good Nursery Guide
- S.Woodford and A.De Zoysa (Vermillion)

How Not To Be a Perfect Mother
- Libby Purves (Fontana)

Mum's the Word
- Jasmine Birtles (O'Mara)

A Parent's Little Instruction Book
- Jasmine Birtles (Boxtree)

Picking the Perfect Nanny
- Jane P.Metzroth (Pocket Books)

NURSERY INTERIOR DESIGNERS

Squidgy Things wants you to feel enchanted every time you enter your child's room.

We use imagination and lots of fun and vibrant colour to create unique, fully co-ordinated interiors which incorporate your own design ideas. We can transform an ordinary room into a captain's ship, a space craft, a fairytale land or an under sea world. In fact, we can create whatever stimulating and colourful environment you choose.

All of our products are hand-crafted and hand-painted from our play and study systems to our recently launched baby basics kit - a custom-made starter kit of furniture at off-the-peg prices. At Squidgy Things we team these with fabrics from the very best British designers. Call us for a catalogue now.

To discuss your ideas, come to our new Knightsbridge showroom or book an appointment for one of our design team to visit your home.

8 Motcomb Street
London SW1X 8JU
Tel: 0171 823 1967
Fax: 0171 823 1976

ALL YOUR 'NURSERY NEEDS'

200 PRAMS AND COTS IN STOCK FOR IMMEDIATE DELIVERY

HIGHCHAIRS   BUGGIES   COTS
CHILDREN'S CLOTHES MOSES BASKETS   COT BEDS
BABYWALKERS   BABYCARRIERS   BEDDING
PUSHCHAIRS   CHANGING UNIT   TRAVEL COTS
SWINGING CRIBS   PRAMS   CAR SEATS

PLUS LARGE SELECTION IN OUR TOY DEPARTMENT

✯ **FREE DELIVERY**
WITHIN OUR DELIVERY AREA
ON ORDERS OVER £100

✯ MAIL ORDER SERVICE &
INFORMATION SERVICE

✯ ONE OF THE LARGEST
INDEPENDENT BABY
EQUIPMENT SUPPLIERS
IN THE UK.

✯ LAYBY/DEPOSIT SERVICE
AVAILABLE - FREE!
TELEPHONE FOR FREE
BROCHURES

ESTABLISHED FOR
OVER 95 YEARS

1901 to 1996

W. J. DANIEL & COMPANY LIMITED

96-122 Uxbridge Road Ealing London W13 8RF Tel: 0181-567 6789 *car park at rear of store*
120-125 Peascod Street Windsor Berks SL4 1DP Tel: 01753 862106
25 Market Place Newbury Berks RG14 5AA Tel: 01635 40017
2-12 City Road Cardiff CF2 3DL Tel: 01222 452894 *car park at rear of store*
1-4 Market Square Ebbw Vale Gwent NP3 6HR Tel: 01495 306656

NANNYTAX

The UK's leading payroll service for parents who employ a nanny

If you employ a nanny you are required by law to register as an employer, keep tax records, and pay Income Tax and National Insurance Contributions to the Inland Revenue - as well as providing payslips for your nanny showing all tax and NI deductions made on her behalf.

Coping with these obligations can prove to be a time-consuming and 'taxing' experience.

We offer a friendly, efficient, *inexpensive* service which takes care of all of your PAYE obligations.

Parents from all walks of life - from film directors and fashion models to doctors and teachers (and even accountants!) - use NANNYTAX.

More than 200 nanny agencies throughout the UK now offer the NANNYTAX service to their clients.

*"I would like to place on record my appreciation of your company and its professionalism. You make simple what could be a nightmare - namely being an employer and having to deal with the Inland Revenue."**

*"Many thanks for your assistance. I very much appreciated the service you provided, especially considering the modest sum that you charge, and would recommend your services highly to friends and relatives."**

*"Thank you for the excellent service you have provided. It has certainly taken the headache out of the accounting and paperwork involved with employing a nanny."**

*"I am very impressed by your high standards of customer care, and grateful for how professional and helpful you've been in enabling me to honour this responsibility**

* a few of the many plaudits received from NANNYTAX subscribers

Please call 01273 626256 for our free brochure or with any queries you may have about becoming an employer - or write to us at P O Box 988, BRIGHTON BN2 1BY

Le Club TRICOLORE

We make French fun!

TRICOLORE *tots* for 2-5 year olds

We play games, sing, paint, cook, read stories
... ALL IN FRENCH!

Le Club for 5-11 year olds

We teach your child practical French:
great fun, good results, plenty of enthusiasm!
Recommended by Daily Telegraph and Good Housekeeping

Party Entertainment ... with a difference!

ZoZo the French clown can 'land' **anywhere** in person
and entertain 3-8 year olds. No knowledge of French required.
Recommended by Tatler, Time Out and Evening Standard Magazine

ZoZo Promotions

We can send you award-winning French games, books
and tapes to entertain and teach children aged 2-11.
Recommended by Times Educational Supplement, Good Toy Guide
Right Start, Daily Mail and Evening Standard Magazine

Holiday Activity Days

Your child can enjoy art and crafts, cookery, games,
singing etc. **in French** during the holidays.
Recommended by Harpers & Queen and Sunday Telegraph.

Find out more!
Call LE CLUB TRICOLORE on 0171 924 4649